ADVOTALK: THE HIDDEN THERAPY

A Self-Healing Guide for People Who Don't Talk

A Delexcare Initiative
by Shola Oyewole

Dedication

To the ones who had to survive without help.
To the ones who had to heal in silence.
To the ones who were told "be strong" when what you really needed was someone to hold you.

This book is for you.

Read This First (Important Disclaimer)

This book is not a replacement for professional mental health care, emergency support, medical advice, or safety planning.

This book is a private space to:

- Understand what hurts
- Find the root of your pain
- Begin healing on your own terms

If you are in danger, feel like hurting yourself or someone else, or feel you cannot stay safe, please contact a crisis hotline, emergency services, or someone you trust immediately.

You matter. Needing help is not weakness.

How to Use This Book

This book is designed like a private session.

Each topic has:

1. **What This Is**
   A plain explanation of the issue.

2. **How It Shows Up in Your Life**
   Behaviors, thoughts, choices, patterns.

3. **Root Questions**
   Deep questions to help you figure out where the pain started.

4. **Release Work**
   A guided writing exercise, visualization, or boundary practice.

5. **Affirmation to Keep**
   Something to repeat until your mind believes it.

This is not homework.
This is not school.
This is for you.

Write in this book. Cry in this book. Argue with this book.
You do not have to be "nice" here. You only have to be honest.

If at any point your body feels tight, your breathing changes, you feel dizzy, shaking, numb, angry, or overwhelmed, pause. Put the book down. Drink water. Touch something solid near you. Remind yourself: "I am here. I am safe right now."

This is slow work. Healing is not a race.

TABLE OF CONTENTS

Dedication 2

Read This First (Important Disclaimer) 3

How to Use This Book 4

INTRODUCTION 8

PART I - WHY YOU HURT 10

CHAPTER 1. WHY YOU DON'T TRUST THERAPY 11

CHAPTER 2. SILENCE BECOMES A HABIT 17

CHAPTER 3. WHAT HAPPENS WHEN PAIN HAS NO NAME 22

PART II - FIND YOUR WOUND 27

CHAPTER 4. ABANDONMENT 28

CHAPTER 5. SHAME 33

CHAPTER 6. FEAR OF LOVE / FEAR OF TRUST 37

CHAPTER 7. THE FATHER WOUND 42

CHAPTER 8. MOTHER WOUND ("I RAISED MYSELF") 45

CHAPTER 9. SEXUAL TRAUMA / BODY BETRAYAL ... 49

CHAPTER 10. EMOTIONAL NEGLECT 52

CHAPTER 11. ANGER AND CONTROL 60

CHAPTER 12. GRIEF & UNFINISHED GOODBYES 63

CHAPTER 13. SELF-BLAME AND GUILT 66

CHAPTER 14. LONELINESS (EVEN WHEN YOU'RE NOT ALONE) 71

PART III — BUILD YOURSELF BACK 76

CHAPTER 15. FEELING SAFE IN YOUR BODY 77

CHAPTER 16. BOUNDARIES WITHOUT GUILT 80

CHAPTER 17. SELF-RESPECT WHEN YOU WERE TRAINED TO SETTLE 83

CHAPTER 18. SOFTNESS AFTER SURVIVAL MODE 86

CHAPTER 19. LEARNING TO RECEIVE LOVE WITHOUT FEAR 90

PART IV — LIVING IN HEALING 93

CHAPTER 20. FORGIVENESS AND LETTING GO 94

CHAPTER 21. RECONNECTING WITH JOY AND PURPOSE 97

CHAPTER 22. CREATING DAILY PEACE ROUTINES .. 100

CHAPTER 23. BECOMING WHOLE AGAIN 103

CLOSING LETTER: YOU MADE IT 105

ACKNOWLEDGMENTS 107

ADVOTALK

RESOURCE & SUPPORT GUIDE 108

INTRODUCTION

Why I Wrote This Book

Some people run to therapy.
Some people run away from therapy.

Let's talk about the second group.

There are people who never felt safe telling their truth because:

- Their pain was used against them.
- They were told "other people have it worse."
- They were called dramatic, angry, damaged, ungrateful, sensitive, weak, crazy, "too much," or "cold."

So they learned silence.

Silence became protection.
Silence became identity.
Silence became "I'm fine."

But here is the truth:
You can lock pain in, and it will still run your life.

It will choose who you date.
It will choose what kind of disrespect you accept.
It will choose how close you allow people to get.
It will choose how angry you get, how fast you shut down, how hard you work to prove yourself, how scared you are of being left.

Pain that is not treated becomes a lifestyle.

That's why this book exists.

This book is not here to judge you.
This book is not here to fix you like you are broken.

This book is here to help you answer the most important question in healing:

Where did it start?

Because without the root, every problem will repeat.

You deserve to understand yourself.
You deserve to stop feeling crazy for reacting the way you react.
You deserve to heal without begging anyone to listen.

This is private healing.
This is honest healing.
This is AdvoTalk.

PART I - WHY YOU HURT

"Before you can heal, you have to understand why you stopped trusting the process of healing."

CHAPTER 1. WHY YOU DON'T TRUST THERAPY

"I've been hurt enough. I'm not telling my story to anyone else."

1. What This Is

Not everyone avoids therapy because they don't believe in it. Many avoid it because they've learned through pain that opening up isn't safe.

Maybe you tried to speak once and were shut down.
Maybe the people who were supposed to listen didn't.
Maybe a "professional" made you feel judged instead of seen.
Maybe you were raised to believe therapy is weakness.
Or maybe you've survived so much that you think no one could possibly understand.

For some, silence feels safer than explaining.
But the truth is: *silence doesn't protect you, it isolates you.*

You don't have to trust therapy to start healing.
You just have to trust **yourself** again, your voice, your body, your story.

2. How This Shows Up in Your Life

- ☐ You hide your emotions because vulnerability feels like exposure.
- ☐ You joke about pain instead of feeling it.
- ☐ You find it hard to believe people genuinely care.
- ☐ You act like nothing affects you, but secretly crave to be understood.
- ☐ You overanalyze every act of kindness, waiting for it to turn into manipulation.
- ☐ You tell yourself "I'm fine" so often that you start believing it.

You don't hate therapy, you hate disappointment.
You hate being vulnerable in front of someone who might not know what to do with your truth.

3. Root Questions

a. When Was the First Time You Felt Unsafe Sharing Your Truth?
Who was it with, and what did they do or say that made you close up?

b. What Do You Fear Most About Opening Up?
Being misunderstood? Being seen as weak? Being rejected?

c. What Would It Take for You to Feel Safe Enough to Talk?
Is it trust? Time? Privacy? Empathy?

d. Who Has Earned the Right to Hear Your Pain — Even a Little?

You don't owe your story to everyone.

But you owe *yourself* the freedom to not keep it locked up forever.

4. Release Work

Exercise: Learning Safe Expression

Instead of diving into therapy right away, start with *yourself*. Open a journal, or even the notes app on your phone, and answer this:

"If I could talk to someone right now, what would I say?"
"What part of my story still hurts to tell?"

Write without editing.
You don't have to share it.
This is your private conversation, your first "session" is with you.

If you cry, it's working.
If you can't write yet, just whisper it in your own space.
You're learning to trust your voice again.

5. Healing Truths

- You can be both skeptical and still deserve help.
- It's okay if therapy didn't work before, you were still worthy of being understood.
- Healing isn't about trusting others first; it's about rebuilding trust with yourself.
- You can take healing one conversation at a time, even if it's on paper.

You don't have to start with a stranger.

You can start right here, by admitting that you're tired of holding everything alone.

6. Keep This With You

Affirmation:

"I am learning to trust my story again.

It's safe to speak.

It's safe to be heard.

And it's safe to heal, even if I start with myself."

DELEXCARE INITIATIVE

CHAPTER 2. SILENCE BECOMES A HABIT

"I learned to hold everything in, because speaking never helped."
"Now I don't even know how to talk about what hurts."

1. What This Is

Silence isn't always peace, sometimes it's protection.
It's what you learn when every time you spoke, you were ignored, punished, or made to feel dramatic.

So you stop talking.
You stop explaining.
You stop asking for help.
You stop expecting to be understood.

You learn to swallow pain until it becomes part of you.
You become "the quiet one," "the strong one," "the one who doesn't talk about feelings."
But deep down, you're screaming, just in a language no one can hear anymore.

You didn't choose silence because you're cold or emotionless.
You chose silence because it was the only way to stay safe.

The problem is, what once protected you is now keeping you trapped.

2. How This Shows Up in Your Life Now

- ☐ You find it hard to express emotions, even good ones.
- ☐ You downplay pain because you don't want to "make it a big deal."
- ☐ You shut down when conversations get deep or uncomfortable.
- ☐ You have a hard time asking for help, even when you desperately need it.
- ☐ You feel misunderstood because people think you "don't care."
- ☐ You use humor or distraction to avoid heavy conversations.

You've learned to carry your feelings quietly, like heavy stones in your pockets,
never letting them show, but feeling their weight every single day.

3. Root Questions

a. When Did You Start Hiding Your Emotions?
Think back, was there a moment, a home, a relationship, or a person who made you feel unsafe expressing yourself?

_____

_____

b. What Were You Taught About Emotions?
Were you told they were weakness? Drama? Sin? Inconvenience?

_____
_____

c. How Do You Punish Yourself for Feeling?
Do you shut down, overwork, isolate, or pretend you don't care?

_____
_____

d. What Emotion Have You Been Silencing the Longest?
Anger? Fear? Sadness? Shame? Longing?
Write it down. Then write what it's been trying to tell you.

_____
_____
_____

4. Release Work

Exercise: Giving Silence a Voice

Sit quietly with yourself.
Imagine your silence sitting across from you, not as an enemy, but as an old friend who once kept you safe.
Say to it (out loud if you can):

"Thank you for protecting me when I didn't have a voice.
But I don't need you to hide my truth anymore.
It's safe to speak now."

Then write freely for five minutes about what your silence has cost you.
No censoring. No grammar. Just truth.

Finish with this sentence:

"My silence kept me safe once, but now it keeps me small."

5. Healing Truths

- Silence can protect you, but it can also isolate you.
- Speaking doesn't always mean talking to others; it can start with writing, crying, praying, or creating.
- Every time you share a truth, even privately, you loosen the grip of shame.
- You don't have to tell the world your story, just stop hiding it from yourself.

Your healing begins when your voice stops whispering and starts existing again.

6. Keep This With You

Affirmation:
"I am learning to speak again, even if my voice shakes.
I am allowed to express what I feel.
Silence protected me once, but truth will heal me now."

CHAPTER 3. WHAT HAPPENS WHEN PAIN HAS NO NAME

"I don't even know what's wrong — I just know something hurts."
"I can't explain it, but it's always there."

1. What This Is

Some pain doesn't have language.
It lives under your skin like background noise, constant, shapeless, familiar.
You can't point to where it began or describe exactly what it feels like.
You just know you've been carrying it for a long time.

This is what happens when emotions were never given words.
When you weren't taught *how* to feel, only *how to cope*.

You learned to say:

- "I'm tired" instead of "I'm depressed."
- "I'm fine" instead of "I'm overwhelmed."
- "I don't care" instead of "I'm scared."

So the pain buried itself deep, nameless but loud, waiting for the day you'd finally recognize it.

You can't heal what you don't understand, but you can start by admitting:

"Something inside me deserves attention."

2. How It Shows Up in Your Life Now

- ☐ You feel emotionally exhausted but can't explain why.
- ☐ You numb out, scrolling, eating, drinking, or staying busy to avoid feeling.
- ☐ You cry easily or get irritated by small things without knowing the real reason.
- ☐ You feel "off" but can't find the words for it.
- ☐ You have physical symptoms, headaches, stomach aches, tightness, with no clear cause.
- ☐ You feel disconnected from joy, purpose, or identity.

That nameless pain isn't weakness, it's a message that's been waiting too long to be heard.

3. Root Questions

a. When Did You First Notice the Weight You Can't Describe?
Try to remember a season, an age, or a moment when you started feeling heavy inside.

b. How Do You Usually Distract Yourself From It?
What do you do to avoid stillness or emotion - work, social media, caretaking, anger, isolation?

c. If Your Pain Could Speak, What Would It Say?
Imagine it has a voice. What would it want you to know?

d. What Feelings Do You Rarely Allow Yourself to Admit?
Shame? Fear? Envy? Regret? Loneliness? Write them down.

Naming your pain doesn't make it bigger, it makes it understandable.

4. Release Work

Exercise: Giving the Pain a Name

Take a blank page and start writing with this sentence:

"The pain I've been avoiding feels like…"

Then describe it however you can, with words, colors, shapes, sensations, or metaphors.
Example: "It feels like a stone in my stomach," or "like fog in my mind."

When you finish, read it slowly.
Then write:

"Now that I've named it, I can begin to heal it."

Keep that page - it's the beginning of your emotional map.

5. Healing Truths

- Pain without language becomes behavior.
  (That's why you shut down, overreact, overwork, or detach - it's pain, not personality.)
- The body remembers what the mouth forgets.
- Naming your pain doesn't mean reliving it; it means reclaiming your control over it.
- When you can identify your feelings, you can start responding to them - not being ruled by them.

You don't need to explain your pain perfectly. You just need to start acknowledging it.

6. Keep This With You

Affirmation:
"I no longer run from what I can't describe.
I am learning to give my pain a name and in doing so, I give myself permission to heal."

PART II - FIND YOUR WOUND

Below are sample chapters to begin your manuscript.

CHAPTER 4. ABANDONMENT

"Why do I always feel like people will leave?"

1. What This Is

Abandonment wounds come from moments or years where you learned that people do not stay.

It can come from:

- A parent physically leaving.
- A parent being present in the house but emotionally unavailable.
- Being passed around (foster care, relatives, "go stay with…").
- Someone you trusted suddenly going silent on you.
- A friend or partner using love like a switch: on, off, on, off.

Abandonment is not only "nobody raised me."
It can also be "people were near me but I never felt chosen."

2. How It Shows Up in Your Life Now

Check all that feel true:

- ☐ I get anxious when someone takes too long to text back.

- ☐ I over-give (money, time, body, loyalty) just so people won't leave me.
- ☐ I stay in relationships that are painful because I'm scared to be alone.
- ☐ I "shut down first" so nobody gets a chance to walk away from me.
- ☐ When people pull back, I start thinking, "What did I do wrong? Why am I not enough again?"
- ☐ I feel like I am always auditioning for love.

If you checked even one, pause. Breathe. You are not dramatic. You are responding to history.

3. Root Questions

Answer in your own words. Be blunt. No filter.

a. First Memory Check

When is the first time you remember feeling like someone important to you chose something/someone else over you?

Write it out:

_____

_____

_____

How old were you? _____

What did you tell yourself about you that day? ("I'm not worth staying for," "I'm too much," "I'm easy to leave," etc.)

DELEXCARE INITIATIVE

_____

b. Pattern Check

Think of the last 2–3 people you got attached to (friend, relationship, even a parent).

For each one:

- Did you feel safe or did you constantly worry they'd leave?
- What did you do to try to "secure" them?

Person 1: _____

What I did to keep them: _____

Person 2: _____

What I did to keep them: _____

Person 3: _____

What I did to keep them: _____

Question for you:
Looking at your answers - did you shrink yourself to avoid being left?

Yes / No / Sometimes. Why?

c. Truth Check

Finish this sentence:
"I am scared that if I stop doing _____ for people, they will leave me."

Write it:

That blank you just filled?
That's not love. That's fear.

4. Release Work

Exercise: "I Am Not Begging You To Stay" Letter

Write a letter (do not send it) to someone who left you or made you feel easy to drop.

Use this frame:

"You leaving taught me _____.
I don't like how it changed me in this way _____.
But I am finished believing that your choice means I am unlovable.
From now on, I will no longer: _____ (list the things you do just to keep people).
I deserve a kind of love that does not feel like a countdown."

Write your full version here:

DELEXCARE INITIATIVE

If you start crying or shaking, that's your survival body letting go of "hold it together." Let it.

5. Keep This With You

Affirmation:
"I am not hard to love.
I was just asking love from people who were not capable of giving it."

Repeat this when you feel that "please don't leave me" panic.

CHAPTER 5. SHAME

"Something is wrong with me."

1. What This Is

Shame is the quiet belief that *you* are the problem.

Not "I did something bad," but "I am bad."

Shame can come from:

- Being blamed for someone else's behavior ("If you didn't act like that, I wouldn't have hit you / cheated / yelled / left").
- Being mocked for your body, your voice, how you cry, how you feel.
- Being told you were dramatic, needy, loud, sensitive, ugly, stupid, annoying.
- Being compared to a "better" sibling.
- Religion or culture used like a weapon instead of guidance.
- Sexual assault or violation that made you feel "dirty."

Shame is powerful because it doesn't just live in your mind. It lives in how you see yourself every single day.

2. How It Shows Up in Your Life Now

Mark what's real for you:

- ☐ I apologize too much for existing. ("Sorry, can I ask a question?" "Sorry, I was just wondering...")

- ☐ Compliments make me uncomfortable. I don't trust them.

- ☐ I feel guilty resting. I only feel valuable when I'm useful.

- ☐ I feel disgust or anger toward my own body.

- ☐ I feel like if people knew the "real me," they would leave.

- ☐ I downplay my pain because I think other people "have it worse."

If you recognize yourself in these, that's not because you're broken. That's because somebody taught you that you needed to earn the right to exist.

That was a lie.

3. Root Questions

a. Who Taught You "You Are The Problem"?
Write a name or role (e.g., "mother," "step-parent," "ex," "church leader," "coach," "family member," "myself").

Who was the loudest voice that made you feel not good enough?

_____

What exact words do you still hear from them in your head? Write them, word for word, even if it hurts:

_____

Now answer this:
If a child said those words to themselves, would you allow it?
Why do you allow it for you?

b. Image Check

When you look at yourself (mirror / photos / voice recordings / how you act around people), what is the first rude comment you think about yourself?

Write it without editing:

Where did that voice come from? You? Or someone else?
Circle one: ME / THEM

If you circled THEM, why are they still allowed to speak in your head?

c. Shame Contract

Finish this sentence honestly:
"I believe I have to be _____ in order to deserve love."

Examples: perfect, quiet, skinny, sexual, useful, smart, obedient, loyal no matter what, funny, unproblematic, strong, independent, never sad, always available.

Write yours:

That line you just wrote? That's your Shame Contract.

You did not sign that contract on purpose. It was forced on you.

You are allowed to begin breaking it.

4. Release Work

Exercise: Break the Contract

Write:
"I release the requirement that I must be _____ to deserve love.
I am allowed to exist as I am, not only as I perform."

Fill it in and rewrite it three times, slowly.

Version 1:

_____

Version 2:

_____

Version 3:

_____

This is how you start re-training your self-worth.

5. Keep This With You

Affirmation:
"I am not 'too much.'
I was just in spaces that asked me to be less."

Say this any time you feel yourself shrinking to make other people comfortable.

CHAPTER 6. FEAR OF LOVE / FEAR OF TRUST

"I want love, but love feels dangerous."

1. What This Is

This wound happens when connection was not safe.

For example:

- You loved someone and they betrayed you.
- You grew up around lies, secrets, cheating, or emotional games.
- You saw "love" used as control.
- You had to earn attention through performance, sex, money, silence, or obedience.
- You were loyal to people who hurt you.
- You saw what love did to someone you care about (for example, you watched your mother, sister, brother, or friend get destroyed by someone they loved).

So now your body learned: closeness = risk.

You think you're "hard to love" or "cold," but you're actually highly alert. You're scanning for disappointment before it happens.

That is survival.

2. How It Shows Up in Your Life Now

Check yourself:

- ☐ I feel uncomfortable when someone is genuinely kind to me.
- ☐ I test people to see if they'll abandon me.
- ☐ When I start to care, I pull back fast.
- ☐ I tell myself "I don't catch feelings," but secretly I want safe love so badly it hurts.
- ☐ I choose emotionally unavailable people so I never have to fully open.
- ☐ I don't believe anyone will love me and stay consistent.

Sometimes you're not "toxic."
You're just scared.

3. Root Questions

a. The First Time Love Hurt You

Think of the first memory where you felt betrayed, used, lied to, embarrassed, or played.

Who was involved (no need to write full name if you don't want):

_____

What happened?

_____

_____

What did you tell yourself about love after that?
Example: "Never trust again," "Don't show feelings first," "Keep one foot out," "Use them before they use you," "Only depend on yourself."

Write yours:

That message became your rulebook in relationships. It's still running.

b. Protection Style
When you start to like someone, what is your first protection move?

- Make them chase you?
- Act colder?
- Get aggressive and start a fight?
- Get clingy and monitor them?
- Shut down sexually or emotionally?
- Pretend you don't care?

Write yours:

Ask yourself:
Is this protecting me, or is this pushing away what I actually want?

c. Trust Check

Finish this sentence:

"I will start to trust someone when I see them do _____ consistently."

Examples: "Tell the truth even when it makes them look bad," "Talk to me with respect when angry," "Show up when I need help," "Keep what I tell them private," "Let me be emotional without making me feel crazy."

Write yours:

_____

This becomes your new trust standard. Not "Are they cute?" Not "Do they like me?"
The real question is: **Can they create safety for me?**

You are allowed to require safety.

4. Release Work

Exercise: The Boundary Promise

Fill this out and read it to yourself every time you feel yourself lowering your standards because you're lonely.

"I promise myself:

1. I will not fight to convince someone to treat me right.
2. I will not beg for clarity.
3. I will not explain basic respect more than once.
4. I will leave anything that feels like anxiety pretending to be love.

5. I will not call chaos 'chemistry.'"

Sign it:

_____ Date: _____

Keep this page. This is how you stop repeating the same heartbreak.

5. Keep This With You

Affirmation:
"My need for love is not weakness.
It is human.
And I deserve the kind of love that does not scare my nervous system."

CHAPTER 7. THE FATHER WOUND

"Why do I keep chasing people who remind me of my father?"

1. What This Is

The *Father Wound* isn't just about whether your father was present.
It's about whether he made you feel seen, safe, and valued.

It can come from:

- A father who left, physically or emotionally.
- A father who was unpredictable - loving one day, distant the next.
- A father who was there but emotionally cold or critical.
- A father who didn't defend you.
- A father who abandoned your mother, leaving you with quiet anger.

When the first man who was supposed to protect you didn't - you internalized it.
You started to believe:

- "I must work hard to be chosen."
- "Love is unstable."
- "Men always leave."
- "I need to prove my worth to be loved."

2. How It Shows Up in Your Life

- ☐ You over-function in relationships — doing everything so they don't leave.
- ☐ You fall for emotionally unavailable people.
- ☐ You crave attention from authority figures or older partners.
- ☐ You don't trust men but still seek their approval.
- ☐ You feel rejected when someone sets boundaries.
- ☐ You're hyper-independent — "I don't need anyone."

3. Root Questions

a. Reflection:
What is your earliest memory of your father or father figure?
Was he gentle, harsh, absent, or unpredictable?
Write what stands out most:

_____

_____

b. Pattern Check:
Think of your romantic relationships.
What behavior reminds you of your father's way of loving?

_____

_____

c. Belief Check:
Complete this:
"Men are _____."

"Love feels like _____."
"The people I love always _____."

Those blanks reveal the story your body still believes.

4. Release Work

Exercise: Reparent Yourself

Write a letter to your younger self from the father you *needed*. Say everything you wish he had said:

"You are enough. I am proud of you. You didn't have to earn my love. I should have protected you. I should have stayed. You never needed to prove your worth to me."

Read this letter out loud when you finish.
It may break you open — that's healing happening.

5. Keep This With You

Affirmation:
"I am not my father's absence.
I am someone who stayed — even when he didn't."

CHAPTER 8. MOTHER WOUND ("I RAISED MYSELF")

"I learned to be the adult before I ever got to be a child."

1. What This Is

The *Mother Wound* is the ache of growing up without emotional safety from the person who was supposed to give it.
It's not about blaming mothers — it's about acknowledging the pain of **not being nurtured, protected, or seen**.

This wound can come from:

- A mother who was physically present but emotionally unavailable.
- A mother who was critical, controlling, or perfectionistic.
- A mother who used guilt or silence instead of affection.
- A mother who made you responsible for her feelings.
- A mother who couldn't love you the way you needed because no one ever loved her that way.

When you are not emotionally mothered, you learn to become your own caretaker too early.
You grow up fast — strong, independent, capable — but deep down, you're still craving a softness you never received.

2. How It Shows Up in Your Life

- ☐ You find it hard to depend on anyone — even when you need help.

- ☐ You feel guilty resting or being vulnerable.

- ☐ You're hyper-independent: "I don't need anyone."

- ☐ You attract people who need fixing, because that's what love used to look like.

- ☐ You're scared of becoming like your mother, yet you catch yourself repeating her patterns.

- ☐ You don't know how to receive affection without discomfort.

You may not even realize you're still parenting yourself and everyone else.

3. Root Questions

a. Childhood Reflection
What was your relationship with your mother like as a child? Was she warm, distant, strict, unpredictable, tired, or emotionally absent?

_____

_____

b. Responsibility Check
At what age did you start feeling like the "adult" in your home? What responsibilities or emotions did you carry that weren't yours?

c. Emotional Inheritance

What lessons did your mother teach you — directly or indirectly — about love, worth, and emotion?
Write what you were told or shown (even through her behavior).

d. The Unspoken Need

If your mother could have given you one thing — a word, a hug, a presence, what would it have been?

That's the need you still try to fill in others.

4. Release Work

Exercise: Re-Mothering the Self

Find a quiet space.
Close your eyes and place your hand on your chest.
Speak to your inner child — the one who never felt nurtured.
Say:

"You didn't have to raise yourself.
You should have been held, protected, and seen.
But I'm here now.
I will take care of you the way you deserved back then."

Now, write a short letter from your adult self to your younger self:
What would you say to that child who had to grow up too soon?

_____

_____

_____

You are not weak for craving care — you were deprived of it.
Now, you have the chance to give it back to yourself.

5. Keep This With You

Affirmation:
"I no longer need to earn love through responsibility.
I am allowed to rest, receive, and be cared for.
The mother I needed — I am becoming her now."

CHAPTER 9. SEXUAL TRAUMA / BODY BETRAYAL

"My body remembers what my mind tries to forget."

1. What This Is

Sexual trauma is not only about the act. It's about **the loss of safety inside your own body.**

It can come from:

- Rape, assault, molestation, or coercion.
- Being touched without consent.
- Sexual comments or objectification as a child or adult.
- Feeling blamed for what happened ("What were you wearing?" "You wanted it.")
- Experiencing shame around sex, even in consensual relationships.

This wound hides in silence, in shame, in the body's tightness and hyper-awareness.

2. How It Shows Up

- ☐ Feeling unsafe being touched, even by people you love.
- ☐ Numbness during intimacy.
- ☐ Flinching or freezing when someone comes close.

- ☐ Oversexualizing yourself to feel in control.
- ☐ Avoiding intimacy completely.
- ☐ Feeling dirty, guilty, or responsible for what happened.

You are not dirty. You were not responsible. You survived.

3. Root Questions

a. Memory and Body Connection:
When you think of that event (or time), where do you feel it in your body — chest, stomach, neck, back, throat?
Write it down:

_____

Your body remembers where your voice was stolen.

b. Trust and Control:
How do you protect yourself now — through control, distance, silence, or pretending?

_____

Has this protection also become a prison?

c. Self-Talk:
What do you secretly say to yourself about that experience?
"I should have known better"? "It's my fault"? "Nobody will believe me"?
Write the truth you wish someone had told you instead:

_____

_____

4. Release Work

Exercise: Reclaiming the Body

Sit somewhere private.
Close your eyes.
Place your hand gently on your heart and say:

"This body is mine.
What happened to me was not my fault.
My body deserves love, comfort, and rest.
I am safe in my body again."

Repeat it daily. You're retraining your nervous system to trust again.

5. Keep This With You

Affirmation:
"I survived what was meant to destroy me.
My body is no longer a battlefield — it is a home I am learning to love."

CHAPTER 10. EMOTIONAL NEGLECT

"Nobody Was There for Me Emotionally."
"I had people around me, but I still felt alone."

1. What This Is

Emotional neglect is when your basic needs were met - food, clothes, school, shelter,
but your emotional needs were ignored.

No comfort.
No softness.
No "How are you really?"
No safe lap to cry on.

You were physically taken care of just enough to survive…
but not emotionally cared for enough to feel loved.

Emotional neglect is quiet trauma.
It's the feeling of growing up in a house where you could not be sad, scared, confused, or overwhelmed without being:

- Shut down

- Ignored

- Dismissed ("You're fine")

- Mocked ("Why are you crying like that?")

- Shamed ("Other kids have it worse")

- Taught to "be strong" before you even knew how to be a child

It's not always that someone "did something to you."
Sometimes it's what they didn't do.

Emotional neglect teaches you:
"My feelings are not important."
"My needs make people uncomfortable."
"It's safer if I keep it to myself."

That belief follows you into adulthood.

2. How It Shows Up in Your Life Now

Check all that feel like you:

- ☐ When I'm upset, I shut down instead of reaching out.

- ☐ I feel like a burden when I ask for help.

- ☐ I hate crying in front of people — it feels dangerous or embarrassing.

- ☐ I say "it's fine" even when it's not fine at all.

- ☐ I don't know how to name what I feel, I just feel "numb" or "off."

- ☐ I have friends/family/partner around me but still feel alone and unsupported.

- ☐ I carry everything by myself because I don't believe anyone will actually show up for me emotionally.

Emotional neglect creates hyper-independence:
"I'll handle it. I always handle it."

But "I'll handle it" is sometimes code for:
"No one else ever did."

3. Root Questions

Be honest. This is private. You don't have to protect anybody here.

a. Growing Up:
When you were sad, scared, overwhelmed, or hurting as a child…
what usually happened?

- Did someone comfort you?
- Were you told to stop crying?
- Were you ignored?
- Were you made to feel dramatic, weak, annoying, "too sensitive"?

Write it in your own words:

_____

_____

_____

b. Message You Learned:
What did that teach you about having emotions?

Complete this sentence honestly:

"I learned that if I show emotion, _____."

That sentence right there is the rulebook you still live by.

c. Today:
Think about the last time you were hurting emotionally.

Who did you want to call or talk to?
Did you stop yourself? Why?

d. Your Pattern in Relationships:
When you're not okay, do you:

- Pretend you're okay so nobody worries?
- Get distant and disappear?
- Get angry instead of vulnerable?
- Overwork/distract so you don't have to feel?
- Cling to someone who gives a little attention even if they're not healthy?

Write the truth:

None of this means you're "cold."
It means no one taught you how to be held.

4. Release Work

Exercise: Teaching Yourself Emotional Safety

You didn't receive emotional safety.
Now you're going to learn how to build it.

Step 1. Write this sentence and finish it:

"Right now, I feel _____."

Example: angry, empty, disappointed, anxious, scared, lonely, tired, forgotten.

Step 2. Ask yourself:

"Why do I feel this way? What happened?"

Write it out like you're talking to someone who actually cares:

_____

_____

_____

Step 3. Give yourself the response you never got.
Say to yourself (out loud if you can):

"It makes sense that you feel this way.
You are allowed to feel this.
You are not too much.
I'm here for you."

Sit with that for a moment.

This may feel weird or fake at first.
It's not fake.
It's new.

Your nervous system has never had this kind of comfort. You're introducing it.

5. Where It Can Hurt You (So You Can Catch It)

Emotional neglect can lead to:

- Choosing emotionally cold partners because it feels "normal."
- Staying quiet in relationships and then exploding later.
- Feeling guilty for having needs.
- Feeling invisible even when loved.
- Feeling chronically misunderstood.

This is why sometimes you're angry, but you're not angry. You're actually lonely.

But you don't know how to say:
"I need you emotionally. I need you to sit with me. I need you to care."

So instead you say nothing… or you say it as anger.

From now on, practice saying the real need:
"I don't need you to fix it. I just need you to stay with me while I feel it."

That is emotional connection. That is repair.

6. Healing Starts With Allowing Yourself to Need

You are allowed to need emotional safety.
You are allowed to want softness.
You are allowed to stop being "the strong one" for once.

Write this to yourself:

"I am worthy of comfort, patience, and gentleness.
I am not a burden for needing love.
I deserve people who can sit with my pain without making me feel guilty for having it."

Write it again in your own voice here:

_____

_____

_____

That becomes your standard.
That becomes your boundary.
That becomes your filter.

If someone cannot meet you emotionally, you are allowed to stop calling it love.

7. Keep This With You

Affirmation:

"I was never 'too emotional.'
I was emotionally unsupported.

From this point on, I honor my feelings.
My emotions matter.
I matter."

ADVOTALK

CHAPTER 11. ANGER AND CONTROL

"I don't know if I'm protecting myself or destroying peace."

1. What This Is

Anger is not bad.
Anger is information, a signal that something feels unsafe, unfair, or unhealed.

But when anger becomes your only language, it's usually because you were never allowed to express softer emotions like sadness, fear, or pain.

You learned: *If I show vulnerability, I'll get hurt.*
So you replaced tears with tension.

2. How It Shows Up

- ☐ You snap easily at small things.

- ☐ You replay arguments in your head long after they're over.

- ☐ You control everything to avoid disappointment.

- ☐ You suppress emotions until you explode.

- ☐ You call it "discipline," but it's really fear of losing control.

- ☐ You avoid apologies because they feel like weakness.

3. Root Questions

a. History Check:
Growing up, what happened when you cried or got angry?
Were you punished, mocked, or ignored?

---

b. Pattern Check:
When you feel threatened now, what's your go-to reaction? (Yelling, silence, cutting people off, working harder, walking away?)

Is this reaction helping or isolating you?

c. Message Underneath the Anger:
Anger often hides a softer truth.
What emotion might live underneath your fear, grief, shame, loneliness?

---

4. Release Work

Exercise: "Speak It Without Fire"

Choose one situation that still makes you angry.
Write this format:

"When you _____, I felt _____.
What I needed instead was _____.
I forgive myself for holding this fire for so long."

This helps you give your anger language instead of destruction.

5. Keep This With You

Affirmation:
"My anger is not my enemy.
It is the voice of the child who wasn't heard."

CHAPTER 12. GRIEF & UNFINISHED GOODBYES

"I never got to say goodbye, and part of me is still there."

1. What This Is

Grief isn't only about death.
It's about **loss** - the loss of a person, a dream, a season, or a version of yourself that will never return.

You can grieve:

- A parent who was alive but emotionally gone.
- A relationship that ended without closure.
- A childhood that wasn't safe or gentle.
- A career, friendship, or community you had to leave behind.
- Even the "old you" who had hope before life changed.

Grief is not weakness. It's proof you once loved deeply.

2. How It Shows Up Now

- ☐ You avoid talking about it because it still hurts.
- ☐ You feel guilty for moving on or being happy.
- ☐ You keep reliving moments that can't be undone.

- ☐ You shut down on anniversaries or holidays.
- ☐ You say "I'm fine" to avoid making others uncomfortable.
- ☐ You feel stuck between acceptance and regret.

If you've been grieving alone, this chapter is your permission to breathe again.

3. Root Questions

a. What Did You Lose?
Name it clearly. Don't soften it to protect yourself.

"I lost _____ and it still hurts because _____."

_____

_____

b. What Was Left Unsaid?
If you could speak to that person or moment one more time, what would you say?

_____

_____

c. What Did You Learn to Hold Inside?
When the loss happened, how did you cope - did you become the "strong one," the "funny one," the "busy one"?

_____

_____

4. Release Work

Exercise: Write the Goodbye You Never Had

Begin with:

"I never got to tell you this but …"

Let your words flow. No grammar, no filter. When you finish, fold the page and say out loud:

"Thank you for what you were. I release what you cannot be anymore."

If it's a person, burn or bury the page safely as a symbol of release.

5. Keep This With You

Affirmation:
"I can miss what's gone and still move forward.
Grief means I loved. And love means there is life left in me."

CHAPTER 13. SELF-BLAME AND GUILT

"It must have been my fault."
"If I had done something differently, maybe things wouldn't have gone wrong."

1. What This Is

Self-blame is what happens when the mind tries to make sense of pain by turning it inward.
It's the quiet logic of a wounded heart:

"If it's my fault, then maybe I could have prevented it."

Guilt, when healthy, helps us take responsibility for what we truly control.
But **toxic guilt** convinces us that everything bad that happens is somehow our doing, even things that were never ours to carry.

This wound often forms when:

- You were blamed for things that weren't your fault.
- You were expected to fix family chaos, even as a child.
- You were punished more for mistakes than you were comforted when you tried your best.
- You were taught to earn forgiveness instead of receiving grace.
- You believed that being "good" would protect you from pain — and it didn't.

So you grew up apologizing for existing.
You became over-responsible for everyone else's emotions while silently abandoning your own.

2. How It Shows Up in Your Life Now

- ☐ You say "I'm sorry" automatically, even when you did nothing wrong.
- ☐ You take responsibility for other people's moods or actions.
- ☐ You replay mistakes in your head for days or years.
- ☐ You struggle to forgive yourself for the past.
- ☐ You minimize your pain because others "have it worse."
- ☐ You can't celebrate wins, you feel guilty being happy.
- ☐ You feel like you must fix everyone to earn love.

You may not realize it, but self-blame keeps you in emotional chains.
It whispers, *"You should have known better,"* when you couldn't have.
It makes you the villain in stories where you were actually the survivor.

3. Root Questions

a. Where Did You Learn to Blame Yourself?
Think back. Who made you feel like mistakes meant you were bad?

_____

_____

b. When Was the First Time You Took Responsibility for Something Beyond Your Control?
(A parent's emotions? A breakup? A loss? A crisis?)

_____

_____

c. What Are You Still Punishing Yourself For?
Be honest. Write the thing you can't stop replaying.

_____

_____

d. If Someone You Loved Went Through the Same Thing, What Would You Tell Them?

_____

_____

Now, notice how much kinder you are to others than to yourself.

_____

4. Release Work

Exercise: Shifting the Blame Back

Take a deep breath and finish this statement aloud:

"It was not my job to _____.
I did not deserve to feel _____.
I was doing my best with what I knew at the time."

Now, write down three things you forgive yourself for today:

1. I   forgive   myself   for
   _____

2. I   forgive   myself   for
   _____

3. I   forgive   myself   for
   _____

Say them slowly.
You may cry. That's the guilt loosening its grip.

5. Truth Reminder

There's a difference between **responsibility** and **burden**.

You are responsible for your growth, not for everyone's happiness.

You are allowed to stop fixing what you didn't break.

When guilt visits again, ask yourself:

"Is this something I can repair, or am I just reliving pain I didn't cause?"

If it's the second one, breathe and release it.

6. Keep This With You

Affirmation:
"I am not the cause of everything that went wrong.
I am the reason I'm still standing.
I forgive myself for surviving the only way I knew how."

CHAPTER 14. LONELINESS (EVEN WHEN YOU'RE NOT ALONE)

"I'm surrounded by people, but I still feel unseen."
"It's like nobody really knows me — not even the ones who say they love me."

1. What This Is

Loneliness isn't about being physically alone.
It's about feeling emotionally disconnected, unseen, unheard, and unvalued, even when others are near.

You can sit in a crowded room, in a relationship, in a family, or in a group chat…
and still feel like a ghost.

Loneliness comes when:

- You hide your true feelings to avoid judgment.
- You play strong because no one seems to notice when you're not okay.
- You keep showing up for others, but no one shows up for you.
- You've been misunderstood for so long that silence feels safer.

It's not that you don't have people.
It's that you don't feel emotionally *met*.

2. How It Shows Up in Your Life Now

- ☐ You feel disconnected even during social events.
- ☐ You scroll through your phone hoping someone will text, but they don't.
- ☐ You downplay your emotions because "no one would get it anyway."
- ☐ You fill your schedule to avoid sitting with the quiet.
- ☐ You feel invisible in your relationships — tolerated, not treasured.
- ☐ You crave deep connection but fear vulnerability.

Loneliness is what happens when the soul keeps whispering,

"See me,"
and nobody looks up.

3. Root Questions

a. When Did You First Feel Invisible?
Think back — was it at home, in school, in a relationship, at church, or in your own family?

_____

_____

b. How Do You Hide Your Loneliness Now?
Do you joke too much, work nonstop, post happy pictures, or disappear for days?

_____

_____

c. Who Makes You Feel Seen - Even for a Moment?
Write one or two names, even if it's rare or brief.

_____

_____

d. What Kind of Connection Do You Actually Long For?
Describe what being "understood" or "held emotionally" looks like to you.

_____

_____

_____

4. Release Work

Exercise: Speaking Into the Silence

Tonight, before bed, speak to yourself the words you wish someone would say.
Use your name. Let it sound like care.

"(Your Name), I see how much you've been carrying.
You don't always have to be the strong one.
You are worthy of love that stays.
You are allowed to be known, not just useful."

Say it out loud - not in your head.
Your nervous system needs to *hear* warmth again.

Now, write a note to your future self:

"The next time I feel lonely, I will remind myself that I am never truly abandoned, I am reconnecting with me."

_____

_____

_____

5. Healing Truths

- Loneliness doesn't mean you're broken, it means you're craving depth.
- The cure for loneliness isn't more people, it's *authentic connection*.
- To be fully seen, you must first stop hiding.

Practice small acts of emotional honesty:
Text someone, "Today was hard."
Say, "I miss you."
Admit, "I'm lonely right now."

Each time you do, you build a bridge back to belonging.

6. Keep This With You

Affirmation:
"I may feel alone, but I am never unseen.

ADVOTALK

I am learning to fill my own silence with gentleness,
and to attract people who can meet me where I truly am."

PART III — BUILD YOURSELF BACK

"Healing isn't who you become after the pain. It's who you remember you were before the pain."

CHAPTER 15. FEELING SAFE IN YOUR BODY

"I don't trust peace, it feels unfamiliar."

1. What This Is

When your body has lived in survival mode for years, peace can feel like danger.
You're used to tension, noise, chaos, not calm.
You confuse *rest* with *boredom*, *silence* with *rejection*, and *safety* with *waiting for something bad to happen*.

This is what trauma does: it teaches your nervous system that danger = normal.

But healing is learning to teach your body something new:
Safety is not the absence of noise - it's the presence of peace.

2. How It Shows Up

- ☐ You can't relax, even when nothing's wrong.
- ☐ You expect bad news when life gets too calm.
- ☐ You overwork or stay busy to avoid your thoughts.
- ☐ Your body feels heavy, restless, or tense for no reason.
- ☐ You're easily startled, anxious, or distracted.

3. Root Questions

a. What Does "Safe" Feel Like?
Describe what safety means to you, not the dictionary version, *your* version.

___

___

b. What Makes You Feel Unsafe?
Is it silence? Eye contact? Intimacy? Being vulnerable?

___

c. What Would It Take to Feel at Ease in Your Own Skin Again?

___

___

4. Release Work

Exercise: Grounding the Body

Whenever you feel overwhelmed:

1. Sit or stand still.
2. Name **5 things you can see, 4 things you can touch, 3 things you can hear, 2 things you can smell, 1 thing you can taste.**
3. Say aloud:

"I am in the present. I survived what happened. I am safe right now."

This re-teaches your body the difference between *then* and *now.*

5. Keep This With You

Affirmation:
"My body is not my enemy.
It is the home I am learning to protect and love again."

CHAPTER 16. BOUNDARIES WITHOUT GUILT

"Saying no makes me feel like a bad person."

1. What This Is

If you grew up having to earn love or keep peace to survive, boundaries feel like betrayal.

You learned:

- Love means self-sacrifice.
- Saying no means rejection.
- Others' comfort matters more than your sanity.

But boundaries aren't walls - they're doors.
You decide who and what comes through.

Boundaries are love in practice.

2. How It Shows Up

- ☐ You say "yes" when you mean "no."
- ☐ You explain yourself too much.
- ☐ You avoid conflict at all costs.
- ☐ You feel guilty for resting or not helping.

- ☐ You fear people will leave if you set limits.

3. Root Questions

a. What Was the First Time You Were Punished for Saying No?

---

b. Who Crosses Your Boundaries the Most Today - and Why Do You Still Allow It?

---

c. What Do You Need to Feel Safe Saying No?

---

4. Release Work

Exercise: The Boundary Sentence

Practice saying this out loud:

"I care about you, but I can't do that right now."
"That doesn't work for me."
"I need time to think about it."
"Please don't speak to me that way."

Then, write your own personal boundary statement below - something you'll start using:

Each time you repeat it, the guilt weakens and self-respect strengthens.

5. Keep This With You

Affirmation:
"My peace is not negotiable.
Boundaries protect what I've healed."

CHAPTER 17. SELF-RESPECT WHEN YOU WERE TRAINED TO SETTLE

"I always end up giving more than I get."

1. What This Is

When life teaches you survival, not self-worth, you settle for crumbs because crumbs used to be better than nothing.

You don't demand more because you fear losing what little you have.
But **respect begins when you stop accepting less.**

Self-respect is not arrogance.
It's remembering your value after being treated like you had none.

2. How It Shows Up

- ☐ You over-explain yourself to people who don't care.
- ☐ You tolerate inconsistency just to feel chosen.
- ☐ You give multiple chances to people who keep proving they don't deserve them.
- ☐ You confuse patience with self-abandonment.
- ☐ You lower your standards to avoid loneliness.

3. Root Questions

a. When Did You First Learn to Shrink?

_____

_____

b. What Have You Accepted Recently That You Know You Didn't Deserve?

_____

c. What Would It Look Like to Respect Yourself Out Loud?
(Think: tone, posture, communication, standards)

_____

_____

4. Release Work

Exercise: The Respect List

Write 5 non-negotiables that define how people must treat you. (Example: No yelling. No ignoring messages. No silent treatment. No manipulation. No excuses.)

1. _____
2. _____
3. _____
4. _____
5. _____

Keep this list. Every time you feel confused about whether to stay or go, look at it.

If they keep breaking your list, they are showing you their truth.

5. Keep This With You

Affirmation:

"I am not difficult. I just no longer tolerate disrespect disguised as love."

CHAPTER 18. SOFTNESS AFTER SURVIVAL MODE

"I'm so used to fighting that peace feels unnatural."
"I don't know how to rest without feeling lazy, or love without feeling unsafe."

1. What This Is

Survival mode is the state your mind and body enter when life demands endurance instead of ease.
It's how you made it through by being alert, guarded, responsible, productive, and always ready for the next crisis.

But healing asks something terrifying:

"Can you stop surviving now?"

You can't go from *hyper-vigilant* to *gentle* overnight.
You've lived too long in "what if."
Softness feels foreign because it was never safe to relax before.

When you've survived chaos, stillness can feel like danger.
When you've always had to protect yourself, vulnerability can feel like weakness.
When you've never had help, comfort can feel suspicious.

This chapter isn't about losing your strength; it's about **redefining it**.

2. How It Shows Up in Your Life Now

- ☐ You keep busy because slowing down triggers anxiety.
- ☐ You only feel valuable when you're achieving something.
- ☐ You struggle to accept love, compliments, or care.
- ☐ You feel tense, even when nothing's wrong.
- ☐ You confuse chaos with purpose.
- ☐ You feel disconnected from emotions - numb, robotic, or "in control."

You survived by staying alert.
Now you're learning to live by staying open.

3. Root Questions

a. What Did You Have to Become to Survive?
List the traits you developed to stay safe - strong, quiet, independent, tough, emotionless, etc.

_____

_____

b. Which of Those Traits Still Serve You?
And which ones are exhausting you now?

_____

_____

c. What Does "Softness" Mean to You?

What images, words, or sensations come to mind when you think of being gentle with yourself?

_____

_____

d. What Are You Afraid Might Happen If You Let Your Guard Down?

_____

_____

That fear is the leftover language of survival.

4. Release Work

Exercise: Practicing Emotional Ease

Find a quiet moment.
Take a deep breath in, hold, and slowly exhale.

Now repeat softly:

"I am safe enough to rest.
I am safe enough to feel.
I am safe enough to soften."

Next, write yourself a permission slip:

"I, _____, give myself permission to stop fighting all the time.
I allow myself to be cared for, to feel joy, and to not have all the

answers.
I am allowed to be gentle with me."

Sign it. Date it.
Place it somewhere you'll see often — it's your new contract with peace.

5. Truths to Remember

- Being soft doesn't mean you're weak; it means you're healing.
- Rest is not laziness, it's restoration.
- You can be powerful and tender at the same time.
- The version of you who fought to survive deserves to rest.

You've mastered strength. Now it's time to learn softness.

6. Keep This With You

Affirmation:
"I no longer need chaos to prove I'm alive.
I can breathe, I can trust, I can rest and still be safe.
Softness is not my weakness. It is my new strength."

CHAPTER 19. LEARNING TO RECEIVE LOVE WITHOUT FEAR

"I want love, but I don't know what to do with it when it shows up."

1. What This Is

When your heart has lived in defense mode, love can feel unsafe.
You might crave closeness but flinch when it arrives.
You might reject affection and later regret it.
You might sabotage healthy people because they don't match your chaos.

That's not brokenness, that's *trauma confusion*.
Your body doesn't trust peace yet.
But you can teach it that good love doesn't hurt.

2. How It Shows Up

- ☐ You overthink when someone is kind to you.
- ☐ You expect rejection after every compliment.
- ☐ You distance yourself when someone gets too close.
- ☐ You mistake calm love for boredom.
- ☐ You crave attention but hate vulnerability.

3. Root Questions

a. What Does "Safe Love" Look Like to You?

List qualities that feel safe, not exciting or dramatic.

---

b. Who Has Given You Gentle Love Before, Even For a Moment?

What did that experience feel like?

---

c. What Do You Fear Will Happen if You Fully Trust Someone?

---

4. Release Work

Exercise: Practicing Receiving

Every day for a week, practice receiving *without explaining or deflecting*.

Examples:

- When someone compliments you, say "Thank you," not "Oh, it's nothing."
- When someone offers help, say "I'd appreciate that."
- When someone shows care, don't question their motive.

After each moment, write how it felt:

You are teaching your nervous system that love is safe again.

DELEXCARE INITIATIVE

5. Keep This With You

Affirmation:
"I am allowed to be loved without earning it.
I am safe in the presence of good love."

PART IV — LIVING IN HEALING

"Healing isn't forgetting what hurt you. It's remembering it without losing yourself."

CHAPTER 20. FORGIVENESS AND LETTING GO

"I'm tired of being angry, but I don't know how to stop."

1. What This Is

Forgiveness is not saying, "What they did is okay."
It's saying, "I deserve peace, and I will no longer carry this pain for them."

You don't have to forgive to please anyone.
You forgive to **free your energy** from resentment.

Forgiveness doesn't erase memory, it removes the poison that keeps replaying it.

2. How It Shows Up

- ☐ You still replay what happened as if it's happening now.
- ☐ You fantasize about closure or revenge.
- ☐ You can't enjoy the present because the past still burns.
- ☐ You're scared that if you forgive, you'll look weak.

3. Root Questions

a. Who Do You Still Think Owes You an Apology?
Write their name(s). Be honest.

b. What Would You Say if You Could Speak Freely?

c. What Has Holding On Cost You (emotionally, physically, mentally)?

4. Release Work

Exercise: The Forgiveness Script

"I may never hear 'I'm sorry,' but I'm releasing the expectation that they'll fix what they broke.
They may never change, but I refuse to keep bleeding for their lesson.
I forgive, not because they deserve peace but because I do."

Write your version in your own voice below:

5. Keep This With You

DELEXCARE INITIATIVE

Affirmation:
"I am not my anger.
I am my release."

CHAPTER 21. RECONNECTING WITH JOY AND PURPOSE

"I forgot what makes me happy."

1. What This Is

When you've lived in pain, joy can feel foreign, even suspicious. You might find yourself asking, *"Am I allowed to smile again?"*

Joy doesn't mean your pain didn't matter.
It means you survived, and now life wants to meet you again.

You are allowed to laugh after trauma.
You are allowed to rebuild meaning from the ashes.

2. How It Shows Up

- ☐ You feel guilty when you're happy.
- ☐ You avoid fun because it feels "fake."
- ☐ You've forgotten your passions.
- ☐ You don't know what to look forward to anymore.

3. Root Questions

a. When Was the Last Time You Felt Free, Even for a Moment?
What were you doing? Who were you with?

b. What Activities, Sounds, or Places Make You Feel Calm or Alive?

c. What Did You Love as a Child Before Life Got Heavy?

4. Release Work

Exercise: The Joy List
Write 10 small things that make your spirit feel light even slightly.

1.
2.
3.
4.
5.
6.
7.
8.
9.
10.

Now promise yourself: Do *at least one* of these every week. Healing without joy is incomplete.

5. Keep This With You

Affirmation:
"I deserve moments that make me smile without apology. Joy is medicine too."

CHAPTER 22. CREATING DAILY PEACE ROUTINES

"How do I keep healing when life gets loud again?"

1. What This Is

Peace is not a one-time event; it's a lifestyle.
It's the daily decision to protect your energy, choose calm, and avoid people who thrive on chaos.

Healing will ask you to build habits that feed your spirit, not your stress.

2. How It Shows Up

Without routines, you'll find yourself repeating pain because chaos feels familiar.
Peace needs structure, not punishment, but rhythm.

3. Root Questions

a. What Are Three Things That Always Disturb Your Peace?

_____

b. What Helps You Reset Fast (prayer, nature, music, writing, etc.)?

_____

c. When Do You Feel Most Grounded — morning, night, or solitude?

_____

_____

4. Release Work

Exercise: Build Your Peace Plan

Create a mini daily routine:

Morning:
What centers you before the world starts?
☐ Prayer / meditation / stretching / gratitude

Midday:
What helps you slow down stress?
☐ Step outside / deep breaths / music / silence

Evening:
What helps you close the day peacefully?
☐ Journaling / forgiveness / soft lighting / affirmations

Write your personal peace plan here:

_____

_____

_____

5. Keep This With You

Affirmation:
"Peace is not found, it is built.
And I am building mine every day."

DELEXCARE INITIATIVE

CHAPTER 23. BECOMING WHOLE AGAIN

"I am no longer surviving, I am living."

1. What This Is

Wholeness is not perfection.
It's integrating every version of you, the broken one, the brave one, the one still learning.

Healing doesn't erase the past; it teaches you how to carry it differently.

You are not "new." You are *realer* than ever.

2. How It Shows Up

- ☐ You respond instead of react.
- ☐ You choose peace over people-pleasing.
- ☐ You no longer chase closure — you create it.
- ☐ You can be alone without being lonely.
- ☐ You forgive yourself for not knowing better before.

3. Root Questions

a. Who Are You Becoming Now That Pain Isn't Driving You?

b. What Parts of You Deserve More Love Moving Forward?

_____

c. What Does "Whole" Feel Like for You, in words, not perfection?

_____

_____

4. Release Work

Exercise: The Mirror Declaration

Stand in front of a mirror. Look directly into your eyes and say:

"I survived.
I'm proud of the person standing here.
I forgive me.
I am becoming the peace I always searched for."

Do this for seven days straight. Watch what changes.

5. Keep This With You

Affirmation:
"I am not healing to forget my story, I am healing to tell it differently."

CLOSING LETTER: YOU MADE IT

Dear Reader,

You've done what most people never do; you looked within.
You faced pain without running.
You spoke to memories that scared you.
You wrote down truths you once buried.

This book was not meant to fix you. It was meant to remind you that you were never broken, only interrupted.

You now have language for what hurt.
You have tools for when your body panics.
You have compassion for the child inside you who didn't get enough love.

Healing doesn't mean you'll never hurt again.
It means when you do, you'll know how to take care of yourself.

As you close this book, remember:
You are your own therapist now.
You are your own safe place.
You are the proof that healing is possible in silence.

Thank you for trusting **AdvoTalk** to walk beside you in this journey.
And when you meet someone who hides behind a smile, hand them this book.
Let them know: *"You're not alone anymore."*

DELEXCARE INITIATIVE

With love,
Shola Oyewole
A Delexcare Initiative

ACKNOWLEDGMENTS

To every survivor who kept going even when no one clapped, this book is for you.

To every person who stayed quiet just to keep peace, you deserve to rest now.

To every reader who dared to face their story, thank you for your courage.

And to those who never found the words, may this book speak for you.

DELEXCARE INITIATIVE

RESOURCE & SUPPORT GUIDE

U.S. & Military Support Lines

- National Suicide Prevention Lifeline (988) — *press 1 for Veterans Crisis Line*

- Crisis Text Line — text **HELLO** to 741741

- National Sexual Assault Hotline — 1-800-656-4673

- National Domestic Violence Hotline — 1-800-799-7233

- SAMHSA Helpline (mental health/substance) 1-800-662-4357

International Readers

Visit [findahelpline.com], which lists global crisis contacts by country

www.ingramcontent.com/pod-product-compliance
Lightning Source LLC
Chambersburg PA
CBHW070205100426
42743CB00013B/3052